G000168045

*Millions of spiritual creatures walk the earth*
*Unseen, both when we wake and when we sleep:*
*All these with ceaseless praise his works behold*
*Both day and night.*

JOHN MILTON

FOR .................................................................

FROM .............................................................

# The GIFT of ANGELS

inspirio

*The gift group of Zondervan*

RUNNING PRESS

PHILADELPHIA · LONDON

Library of Congress Control Number: 2003100939

Running Press ISBN 978-0-7624-1681-3
Zondervan ISBN 0-310-80632-1

This book may be ordered by mail from the publisher. Please
include $1.00 for postage and handling.
*But try your bookstore first!*

Running Press Book Publishers
2300 Chestnut Street
Philadelphia, PA 19103-4371

Visit us on the web!
www.runningpress.com
www.inspiriogifts.com

# CONTENTS

# BIBLICAL TRUTHS
*about Angels*

- The ministry of holy angels will never contradict the Bible.

- The actions of holy angels will always be consistent with the character of Christ.

- A genuine encounter with a holy angel will glorify God, not the angel. Holy angels never draw attention to themselves. They typically do their work and disappear.

# INTRODUCTION

Angels and their interactions with human beings are an integral part of the Bible text. They are mentioned 294 times in more than half the biblical books. The Scriptures record the activities of angels serving as warriors, guardians, deliverers, messengers, instruments of praise and worship to God, facilitators of God's judgments, and ministers to mankind. We are told that these heavenly beings are invisible spirit beings created by God for his service.

Within these pages, we have worked to illuminate the nature and characteristics of biblical angels, both through biblical accounts and stories of encounters with angels by everyday people just like you. We hope that as you read, you will see the truth—that angels are ever among us—and rejoice in this mighty gift of God.

# ANGELS SERVE
## *as Guardians*

*The LORD will command his angels*
  *concerning you*
*to guard you in all your ways;*
*they will lift you up in their hands,*
*so that you will not strike your foot*
  *against a stone.*

PSALM 91:11–12

*The LORD said, "See, I am sending an*
*angel ahead of you to guard you along the*
*way and to bring you to the place*
*I have prepared."*

EXODUS 23:20

## SAFE FROM THE HAND OF HEROD

After Jesus was born in Bethlehem in Judea, during the time of King Herod, Magi from the east came to Jerusalem and asked, "Where is the one who has been born king of the Jews? We saw his star in the east and have come to worship him."

When King Herod heard this he was disturbed, and all Jerusalem with him.

When he had called together all the people's chief priests and teachers of the law, he asked them where the Christ was to be born. "In Bethlehem in Judea," they replied, "for this is what the prophet has written. . . ."

Then Herod called the Magi secretly and found out from them the exact time the star had appeared. He sent them to Bethlehem and said, "Go and make a careful search for the child. As soon as you find him, report to me, so that I too may go

13

and worship him."

After they had heard the king, they went on their way, and the star they had seen in the east went ahead of them until it stopped over the place where the child was. When they saw the star, they were overjoyed. On coming to the house, they saw the child with his mother Mary, and they bowed down and worshipped him. Then they opened their treasures and presented him with gifts of gold and of incense and of myrrh. And having been warned in a dream not to go back to Herod, they returned to their country by another route.

When they had gone, an angel of the Lord appeared to Joseph in a dream. "Get up," he said, "take the child and his mother and escape to Egypt. Stay there until I tell you, for Herod is going to search for the child to kill him."

So he got up, took the child and his mother during the night and left for Egypt, where he stayed until the death of Herod.[1]

*Everlasting God:*
*You have ordained and constituted—in a*
*wonderful order—the ministries of angels*
*and mortals: Mercifully grant that, as your*
*holy angels always serve and worship you*
*in heaven, so by your appointment they*
*may help and defend us here on earth;*
*through Jesus Christ our Lord, who lives*
*and reigns with you and the Holy Spirit,*
*one God, for ever and ever. Amen.*

BOOK OF COMMON PRAYER

*If you pray truly, you will feel within
yourself a great assurance: and the
angels will be your companions.*

EVAGRIUS OF PONTUS

*Jacob also went on his way, and the
angels of God met him. When Jacob saw
them, he said, "This is the camp of God!"
So he named that place Mahanaim.*

GENESIS 32:1–2

# MIDNIGHT VISITOR

A young widow speaks of a time shortly after the death of her husband. Left to raise six children on her own, she depended heavily on family for support. With people around most of the day and plenty of work, she appeared brave. But after the children were all asleep in their beds and the house was quiet, fear would well up in her.

Each night she would lock the doors, and latch the windows, and turn on her bedside lamp to read. But she couldn't seem to conquer the fear and worry that crawled up under the quilt beside her. Everyday house noises amplified themselves. Every creak or rustling became a burglar with a weapon.

Reason flew out the window when fear settled in. Usually the young widow would read longer than she could afford to and then fall asleep with the lamp burning. No matter how she tried, she could not talk faith into her faltering heart.

"God," she prayed one night before finally dozing off, "I know I should not be fearful. I know the Bible says you will never forsake me, but I cannot see you. I cannot feel safe. Please, God, reassure me."

The widow awoke about midnight and lay awake, sensing that someone was in the room. There at the foot of the bed stood a tall man. He did not speak, and she did not speak. Oddly, she felt no fear at all. The widow stared at him, and he nodded slightly. She knew he was not really a man, but her very own guardian angel—the answer to her prayer.

She turned over and went back to sleep peacefully. Though she never saw the angel again, she knew he was there, watching over her and her children. Nighttime never again held her in a grip of fear and dread.[2]

The Gift of Angels

*Dear Angel ever at my side,*
*How lovely you must be*
*To leave your home in heaven*
*To guard a one like me.*

AUTHOR UNKNOWN

*The LORD placed on the east side of the*
*Garden of Eden cherubim and a flaming*
*sword flashing back and forth to guard the*
*way to the tree of life.*

GENESIS 3:24

Angels Serve as Guardians

*Hush! My dear; lie still and slumber;*
*Holy angels guard thy bed.*
*Heavenly blessings without number*
*Gently falling on thy head.*

ISAAC WATTS

*When the servant of the man of God got*
*up and went out . . . an army with horses*
*and chariots had surrounded the city.*
*"Oh, my lord, what shall we do?" the*
*servant asked.*
*"Don't be afraid," the prophet answered.*

# The Gift of Angels

*"Those who are with us are more than
those who are with them."
And Elisha prayed, "O LORD, open his
eyes so he may see." Then the LORD opened
the servant's eyes, and he looked and saw
the hills full of horses and chariots of fire
all around Elisha.*

2 KINGS 6:15–17


*An angel is a spiritual creature created by
God without a body, for the service of
Christendom and of the Church.*

MARTIN LUTHER

*Sleep, my child and peace attend thee,*

*All through the night;*

*Guardian angels God will lend thee,*

*All through the night;*

*Soft the drowsy hours are creeping,*

*Hill and dale in slumber steeping,*

*Love alone his watch is keeping—*

*All through the night.*

OLD WELSH AIR

# ANGELS DELIVER US
## *from Harm*

*The angel of the LORD encamps
  around those who fear him,
and he delivers them.*

PSALM 34:7

*What's impossible to all humanity
may be possible to the metaphysics
and physiology of angels.*

JOSEPH GLANVILLE

*Christians should never fail to sense the operation of angelic glory. It forever eclipses the world of demonic powers, as the sun does a candle's light.*

BILLY GRAHAM

*Our forefathers went down into Egypt, and we lived there many years. The Egyptians mistreated us and our fathers, but when we cried out to the LORD, he heard our cry and sent an angel and brought us out of Egypt.*

NUMBERS 20:15–16

# The Gift of Angels

*The angels are the dispensers and administrators of the Divine beneficence toward us; they regard our safety, undertake our defense, direct our ways, and exercise a constant solicitude that no evil befall us.*

JOHN CALVIN

*The angel of God, who had been traveling in front of Israel's army, withdrew and went behind them. The pillar of cloud also moved from in front and stood behind them, coming between the armies of Egypt and Israel. Throughout the night the cloud brought darkness to the one side and light to the other side; so neither went near the other all night long.*

EXODUS 14:19–20

# GOD'S ANGEL IN THE FIERY FURNACE

King Nebuchadnezzar leaped to his feet in amazement and asked his advisers, "Weren't there three men that we tied up and threw into the fire?"

They replied, "Certainly, O king."

He said, "Look! I see four men walking around in the fire, unbound and unharmed, and the fourth looks like a son of the gods."

Nebuchadnezzar then approached the opening of the blazing furnace and shouted, "Shadrach, Meshach and Abednego, servants of the Most High God, come out! Come here!"

So Shadrach, Meshach and Abednego came out of the fire . . . the fire had not harmed their bodies, nor was a hair of their heads singed; their robes were not scorched, and there was no smell of fire on them.

Then Nebuchadnezzar said, "Praise be to the God of Shadrach, Meshach and Abednego, who has sent his angel and rescued his servants!"[3]

The Gift of Angels

*In all the distress of his people the*
     LORD *too was distressed,*
*and the angel of his presence saved them.*
*In his love and mercy he redeemed them;*
*he lifted them up and carried them*
*all the days of old.*

ISAIAH 63:9

*Today I stumbled and once again*
*Was lifted up by an unseen hand*
*What comfort and joy that knowledge brings.*
*For I hear the whisper of angel wings.*

AUTHOR UNKNOWN

*The golden moments in the stream of life rush past us and we see nothing but sand; the angels come to visit us, and we only know them when they are gone.*

GEORGE ELIOT

## CAUGHT ON THE TRACKS

Marie and Anne had spent six wonderful weeks in Europe and were now capping off their trip with a visit to Marie's brother, who was on assignment in Naples. By the time the women reached the city, they thought of themselves as seasoned travelers. Their Eurrail passes were used up, but they felt confident enough to rent a car. Just in case, they practiced in a nearby neighborhood before navigating the streets. Their rented Fiat was slow but steady, and they felt they would do just fine.

Anne was driving when the women suddenly found themselves caught in a maelstrom of honking cars. They were headed for the bay and could see the turquoise water off in the distance. But to get there, they would have to make several difficult maneuvers. First, they would have to cross two lanes of traffic, then enter an open steel door to cross two lanes of street car tracks, then exit through another open steel door, before getting onto the bay drive.

The women negotiated the traffic lanes without incident and made it through the first open steel door and onto the tracks.

But then they were confronted by a terrible sound. WHRUMP! The car stopped on the tracks and both steel doors swung shut, locking them in! A streetcar was coming toward them, moving very fast. The last thing the women remember seeing was the terrified look of the streetcar driver. Then they closed their eyes and waited for the inevitable.

The women heard a gentle *whoosh* sound and then looked up to see that their car was now on the bay drive. Both steel doors were still closed and locked behind them. Through the partially open car window, Marie heard a pedestrian say to a companion, "Did you see what just happened? It's a miracle!"

Marie and Anne cannot explain what happened to them that day on the streets of Naples. All they can say for sure is that their confidence in themselves failed them, while their confidence in God and his mighty guardian angels was established for all time.[4]

*Angels, angels, so very strong,*
*Obeying God's Word, even in song.*
*They are ready and alert for me,*
*Should I summon them on bended knee.*

*Angels, angels, flames of fire,*
*Delivering God's message, awe to inspire*
*Doing His bidding whenever He calls,*
*Subduing the enemy, giving us pause.*

BETSY WILLIAMS[5]

# Angels Deliver Us from Harm

*I am convinced that these heavenly beings
exist and that they provide unseen aid on
our behalf . . . I believe in angels because the
Bible says there are angels; and I believe the
Bible to be the true Word of God.*

BILLY GRAHAM

*I know that God is watching me
And sees the danger I can't see;
And in my very darkest hour
He sends his angels full of power
To guard me though I'm unaware
That they are even standing there.*

## The Gift of Angels

*God's angels guard me in life's way*
*And camp around me night and day.*

ED STRAUSS[6]

*Jesus said, "See that you do not*
*look down on one of these little ones.*
*For I tell you that their angels*
*in heaven always see the face of*
*my Father in heaven."*

MATTHEW 18:10

## Angels Deliver Us from Harm

*Jesus said, "Do you think I cannot
call on my Father, and he will
at once put at my disposal more
than twelve legions of angels?"*

MATTHEW 26:53

*Angels are the undercover agents God
assigned to protect his children.*

BETSY WILLIAMS

# The Gift of Angels

*You are never alone. Your guardian angel is right beside you always ready to help at the slightest need.*

AUTHOR UNKNOWN

*At once the Spirit sent Jesus out into the desert, and he was in the desert forty days, being tempted by Satan. He was with the wild animals, and angels attended him.*

MARK 1:12–13

*Every redeemed one will understand the ministry of angels in their own life. The angel who was their guardian from their earliest moment; the angel who watched their steps and covered their head in the day of peril, the angel who was with them in the valley of the shadow of death, who marked their resting place, who was the first to greet them in the resurrection morning—what will it be to hold conversation with them, and to learn the history of divine interposition in the life, of heavenly cooperation in every work for humanity!*

E. B. WHITE

*T*he high priest and all his associates, who were members of the party of the Sadducees, were filled with jealousy. They arrested the apostles and put them in the public jail. But during the night an angel of the Lord opened the doors of the jail and brought them out. "Go, stand in the temple courts," he said, "and tell the people the full message of this new life."

ACTS 5:17–20

# ANGELS SERVE
## *as Messengers*

*The word "angel" simply means "messenger."*

DAN SCHAEFFER

*Angels from the realms of glory,*
*Wing your flight o'er all the earth.*
*Ye who sang creation's story,*
*now proclaim Messiah's birth:*
*Come and worship,*
*Come and worship,*
*Worship Christ the newborn King.*

JAMES MONTGOMERY

# The Gift of Angels

*It came upon the midnight clear,*
*That glorious song of old,*
*From Angels bending near the earth*
*To touch their harps of gold;*
*"Peace on the earth, good will to man*
*From Heaven's all gracious King."*
*The world in solemn stillness lay*
*To hear the angels sing.*

EDMUND HAMILTON SEARS

*God will deign to visit oft the*
   *dwellings of just men,*
*Delighted, and with*

*frequent intercourse*
*Thither will send his winged messengers*
*On errands of supernal grace.*

JOHN MILTON

# THE ANGEL GABRIEL
# DELIVERS A MESSAGE
# TO MARY

In the sixth month, God sent the angel
Gabriel to Nazareth, a town in Galilee,
to a virgin pledged to be married to a man

named Joseph, a descendant of David. The virgin's name was Mary. The angel went to her and said, "Greetings, you who are highly favored! The Lord is with you."

Mary was greatly troubled at his words and wondered what kind of greeting this might be. But the angel said to her, "Do not be afraid, Mary, you have found favor with God. You will be with child and give birth to a son, and you are to give him the name Jesus. He will be great and will be called the Son of the Most High. The Lord

God will give him the throne of his father
David, and he will reign over the house of
Jacob forever; his kingdom will never end."

"How will this be," Mary asked the
angel, "since I am a virgin?"

The angel answered, "The Holy Spirit
will come upon you, and the power of
the Most High will overshadow you. So
the holy one to be born will be called the
Son of God. Even Elizabeth your relative
is going to have a child in her old age,
and she who was said to be barren is in

her sixth month. For nothing is impossible with God."

"I am the Lord's servant," Mary answered. "May it be to me as you have said." Then the angel left her.[7]

## AN ANGEL ANNOUNCES THE RESURRECTION

After the Sabbath, at dawn on the first day of the week, Mary Magdalene and the other Mary went to look at the tomb.

Angels Serve as Messengers

There was a violent earthquake, for an
angel of the Lord came down from heaven
and, going to the tomb, rolled back the
stone and sat on it. His appearance was like
lightning, and his clothes were white as
snow. The guards were so afraid of him
that they shook and became like dead men.

The angel said to the women, "Do not
be afraid, for I know that you are looking
for Jesus, who was crucified. He is not
here; he has risen, just as he said. Come
and see the place where he lay."[8]

# The Gift of Angels

*Around our pillows golden ladders rise,*
*And up and down the skies,*
*With winged sandals shod,*
*The angels come and go, the*
   *Messengers of God!*

RICHARD HENRY STODDARD

*Jacob had a dream in which he saw a*
*stairway resting on the earth, with its top*
*reaching to heaven, and the angels of God*
*were ascending and descending on it.*

GENESIS 28:12

# ANGEL IN A KHAKI SUIT

John went out that morning headed into town to the bank. Ida stayed behind at home. She hated to get out in such bitter weather. It was a good twelve and a half miles to town.

"A man kind of needs to get out of the house sometimes," John said aloud to himself. He had tuned his radio to Paul Harvey's "The Rest of the Story" when he spotted a man standing off to the side of the road ahead.

Well, John was not uncaring, but he never picked up hitchhikers, just never! His outspoken opinion was that a man walking is walking for a reason. If he's got trouble, walking might just be the best thing for him—give him air, stretch his legs, and his mind, and maybe help him work things out.

This man had stopped and turned to look back at John. He didn't raise his thumb—just stood, staring. His stance seemed odd. John suddenly felt that he must stop, that he should offer the stranger a ride. He pulled over.

"Going into town?" John called out to him. "Climb on in, man. It's a nasty day to be out without a jacket." The fellow was dressed in a brown khaki shirt and khaki pants.

"Thanks," he responded, "It is nippy, that wind. I'm needing to get to a parts store. My car's on the fritz again." He settled into the seat of the truck, and John offered him a handshake.

The Gift of Angels

"Are you a Christian?" the passenger asked suddenly.

"Yes, in fact I am. I'm a charter member of Country Creek Baptist," John replied. "And you?"

"Me? I'm a member of the Church of God," he said confidently.

They talked more about God as they drove into town. Dropping his rider off at the parts store, John went on to the bank. Finishing that errand, he pulled into the Winn Dixie to pick up a few items for

Ida: milk, bread, and a bag of candy orange slices, you know that gummy kind with the sugar on the outside. Then he swung back by the parts store. Mr. Khaki Suit was just coming out and smiled broadly when he saw John had stopped by for him.

"Gosh, man, you didn't need to worry about me," he said as he slid into the seat.

"I thought I'd run you back out to your car," John explained. "You can get it back on the road and get on your way home."

"'Preciate the kindness," came the soft answer.

They drove out of town nearly eight miles. As they drove, the man talked to John about Jesus. "He'll be coming back soon. Get ready," he said.

"You can let me out here." The man spoke suddenly.

No vehicle was in sight. "I'm in no hurry," said John. "I can run you to your car. How much further is it?"

"No, no," the man said. "Right here

will be just fine."

"Here?" John queried as he looked around for some sign of the phantom car.

"Yessiree. This is good," the man said.

"If you say so, Brother." John pulled off the road and as the stranger opened the door added, "Here, take this bag of candy. Something to munch on while you work."

"Thanks man! One of my all time favorites," the man said and closed the door. John looked ahead to see if he could spot the car anywhere off the road. He saw nothing. He looked back. The man in the khaki suit was nowhere to be seen.

The next week, John stopped at the Crossing Café for a cup of coffee and told his friends there about the man he had met.

Millie was waiting tables and when John mentioned the khaki suit, she gasped and then tears came to her eyes.

"Joe was in here earlier," she said. "He told me he'd picked up a hitchhiker wearing a khaki outfit. The guy told Joe that Jesus was coming back soon, and he should get ready. Joe says he turned his head for just a minute, and when he turned back, the man was gone from the cab of the truck. Another strange thing. Joe says the guy left behind a bag of orange slice candy on the seat—you know that gummy kind with the sugar on them?"[9]

# ANGELS MINISTER
## to Our Needs

*Are not all angels ministering spirits sent to serve those who will inherit salvation?*

HEBREWS 1:14

*Angelic beings are continually ministering to people in many ways in these present days. Many seeming coincidences are really angels on the job!*

ROLAND BUCK

# AN ANGEL MINISTERS TO JESUS

Jesus went out as usual to the Mount of Olives, and his disciples followed him. On reaching the place, he said to them, "Pray that you will not fall into temptation." He withdrew about a stone's throw beyond them, knelt down and prayed, "Father, if you are willing, take this cup from me; yet not my will, but yours be done." An angel from heaven

appeared to him and strengthened him.
And being in anguish, he prayed more
earnestly, and his sweat was like drops of
blood falling to the ground.[10]

*Remember to welcome strangers in your
homes. There were some who did that and
welcomed angels without knowing it.*

HEBREWS 13:2 GNT

*Angels descending, bring from above,
Echoes of mercy, whispers of love.*

FANNY J. CROSBY

*The angels may have wider spheres of action and nobler forms of duty than ourselves, but truth and right to them and to us are one and the same thing.*

EDWIN HUBBELL CHAPIN

## MAILBOX ANGEL

The card came in the mail one simmering hot summer morning. No one expected it, least of all the Hollingworths.

Liz was good at making do. She'd been

finding ways to get by for quite some time. But with each passing day, the challenge seemed to grow bigger. The problem was a precious baby boy born with a heart defect that required surgery shortly after his birth. He was recovering much to Liz's and Rob's great joy, but the medical bills continued to flood in. It seemed like each day some doctor or service had to be added to the pile.

Liz and Rob struggled to keep the mortgage paid, nutritious food on the table, and the utilities paid. They managed without new shoes and clothes. And the food budget was stretched with beans and rice. The couple and their older children tilled up most of backyard and planted a garden of peas, tomatoes and squash to help the family through the spare days. Still the family barely got by.

The card came early one afternoon. Liz sat down on the porch steps and looked at it for a while. She never hurried to open mail. Most of it was bills anyway.

But this card seemed different. The address was hand written and there was no return address—only a postmark that read Depew, Oklahoma. The town was about an hour away, located beside a forsaken but once-busy thoroughfare bypassed by the turnpike. Who did she know there? No one. Not one single person.

Liz opened the envelope, unsealing the goldfish symbol on the back flap, and marveled at what she saw. The front of the card featured an angel in flight—a

rather Americanized angel in a patchwork
gown with quilted wings. A pair of sandals
graced her feet and a tin ring of a halo
attempted unsuccessfully to hold her hair
down. Blond wisps of hair curled and
streamed back behind her in the wind.
Inside, Liz found a short poem—a cou-
plet: "For buttons and bows and shoes
for your toes," accompanied by gift certificates to a Wal-Mart store. Each $50.00
certificate was addressed to one of the
children with a larger amount for Liz and

her husband. The certificates were signed "Your Guardian Angel."

Liz held the card to her heart and cried for joy. She knew the hospital bills would continue to pile up on the desk inside. But something had changed inside her heart. She felt this gift was a down-payment of sorts. In his way, in his time, God would minister to all their needs.[11]

Angels Minister to Our Needs

*In this dim world of clouding cares,*
*We rarely know, till 'wildered eyes*
*See white wings lessening up the skies,*
*The angels with us unawares.*

GERALD MASSEY

## ANGELS TELL US
### *about the Future*

*Angels mean messengers and ministers.*
*Their function is to execute the plan of*
*divine providence, even in earthly things.*

SAINT THOMAS AQUINAS

# The Gift of Angels

*Angels are spirits, but it is not because they are spirits that they are angels. They become angels when they are sent. For the name angel refers to their office, not their nature. You ask the name of this nature, it is spirit; you ask its office, it is that of an Angel, which is a messenger.*

SAINT AUGUSTINE

*"Then I saw another angel flying high in the air, with an eternal message of Good News to announce to the peoples of the earth, to every race, tribe, language, and*

*nation. He said in a loud voice, "Honor*
*God and praise his greatness! For the time*
*has come for him to judge all people.*
*Worship him who made heaven, earth,*
*sea, and the springs of water!"*

REVELATION 14:6–7 GNT

# AN ANGEL TELLS PAUL
# WHAT WILL HAPPEN

Paul stood up before them and said:
"Men, you should have taken my
advice not to sail from Crete; then you

would have spared yourselves this damage and loss. But now I urge you to keep up your courage, because not one of you will be lost; only the ship will be destroyed. Last night an angel of the God whose I am and whom I serve stood beside me and said, 'Do not be afraid, Paul. You must stand trial before Caesar; and God has graciously given you the lives of all who sail with you.' So keep up your courage, men, for I have faith in God that it will happen just as he told me."[12]

# WORDS OF
# RECONCILIATION

M ichele was roused out of a deep
sleep by the sense of someone
standing over her. What she saw was an
incredible sight, a radiant angel at the
side of her bed.

He didn't say, "Don't be afraid," but all
the same she felt no fear. His voice was
deep and as warm as the sun. "You need to
know your father is dying," the angel said.

He lingered a moment, as if to give Michele time to consider his words. Then he drew back and was gone.

Michele hadn't seen her mother in the last year and hadn't seen much of her father. Her mother had trouble accepting Michele's husband and would never attend family events that included his parents or siblings. Things had come to a bitter standoff.

Pondering the message the angel had brought her, Michele wondered what God wanted her to do now. For years, any gesture of kinship she made was futile—finally she had given up. Did God mean for her to reach out again? Why would her efforts be received differently now? She wondered if her parents even knew of her father's dire situation.

With Christmas just around the corner, Michele decided to invite her parents to the family celebration that would be held in her home, scarcely expecting them to come. To her surprise—and joy—they did. Suddenly, barriers that had separated the family for so long seemed to be coming down. A bridge to reconciliation was being forged.

A few weeks later, Michele's mother called to tell her that her father was sick. A doctor's visit in February brought the diagnosis—lung cancer.

Michele was thankful that she had acted on the angel's message from God to her. She knew that, soon, her mother would need help to care for her father, and now she could offer help.

Michele's father died in June that year. With the care of his family, he was able to spend those last months at home, as he wished, instead of in a hospital.

Michele will always cherish those days—gifts really—given to her by the Lord, through the words of an angel.[13]

*The Scripture says there is a time to be born and a time to die. And when my time to die comes, an angel will be there to comfort me. He will give me peace and joy even at that most critical hour and usher me into the presence of God, and I will dwell with the Lord forever. Thank God for the ministry of his blessed angels.*

BILLY GRAHAM

# THE ANGEL OF THE LORD
# FORETELLS OF SAMSON

T he angel of the LORD appeared to Manoah's wife and said, "You are sterile and childless, but you are going to conceive and have a son. Now see to it that you drink no wine or other fermented drink and that you do not eat anything unclean, because you will conceive and give birth to a son. No razor may be used on his head, because the boy is to be

a Nazirite, set apart to God from birth,
and he will begin the deliverance of Israel
from the hands of the Philistines."[14]


*The revelation of Jesus Christ, which God
gave him to show his servants what must
soon take place. He made it known by
sending his angel to his servant John.*

REVELATION 1:1

# ANGELS
## *Worship God*

*Praise the LORD, you his angels, you mighty ones who do his bidding, who obey his word.*

PSALM 103:20

*We praise thee, O God: we acknowledge thee to be the Lord.*
*All the earth doth worship thee: the Father everlasting.*
*To thee all Angels cry aloud: the Heavens, and all the Powers therein.*
*To thee Cherubin, and Seraphin: continually do cry,*

The Gift of Angels

*Holy, Holy, Holy: Lord God of Sabaoth;*
*Heaven and earth are full of the Majesty:*
*    of thy Glory.*

MORNING PRAYER TE DEUM

# ANGELS SURROUND THE THRONE OF GOD

I [the Apostle John] saw an open door in heaven. And the voice that sounded like a trumpet, which I had heard speaking to me before, said, "Come up here, and I will show you what must happen after this." At once the Spirit took control of me. There in heaven was a throne with someone sitting on it. His face gleamed like such precious stones as jasper and carnelian, and all around the throne there was a rainbow the color of an emerald. In a circle around the throne were twenty-four other thrones, on which were seated twenty-four elders dressed in white and wearing crowns of gold. From the throne came flashes of lightning, rumblings, and peals of thunder. In front of the throne seven lighted torches were burning, which are the seven spirits of God. Also in front of the throne there was what looked like a sea of glass, clear as crystal.

Surrounding the throne on each of its sides, were four living creatures covered with eyes in front and behind. The first one looked like a lion; the second looked like a bull; the third had a face like a human face; and the fourth looked like an eagle in flight. Each one of the four

living creatures had six wings, and they
were covered with eyes, inside and out.
Day and night they never stop singing:

"Holy, holy, holy, is the

Lord God Almighty,

who was, who is, and who

is to come."

The four living creatures sing songs
of glory and honor and thanks to the one
who sits on the throne, who lives forever
and ever. When they do so, the twenty-four
elders fall down before the one who sits on

the throne, and worship him who lives forever and ever. They throw their crowns down in front of the throne and say,

"Our Lord and God! You are worthy to receive glory, honor, and power. For you created all things, and by your will they were given existence and life."[15]

# Angels Worship God

*Angels, help us to adore Him;*
*Ye behold Him face to face;*
*Sun and moon, bow down before Him,*
*Dwellers all in time and space.*
*Alleluia! Alleluia!*
*Praise with us the God of grace.*

HENRY FRANCIS LYTE

*Praise the LORD from the heavens,*
*    praise him in the heights above.*
*Praise him, all his angels,*
*    praise him, all his heavenly hosts.*

PSALM 148:1–2

# THE TABERNACLE OF GOD

Sheila was basically a homebody. She had traveled very little and never out of the United States. That's why signing up for a trip to Mexico to help a small congregation build a church was such a big step of faith.

"I won't kid you," Pastor Burkhardt told her. "It's a lot of hard work. We put in long days, pouring cement, laying brick, but every minute is worth it. The people

Angels Worship God

are so kind and good. It's a pleasure to help them. A trip like this can change you forever." Pastor's words and her friends who had been on previous trips finally convinced Sheila to step out in faith and try something new.

Sheila tried many times to imagine what the small village would look like. But when the bus finally pulled up, she couldn't believe it. The main street was muddy from recent rains. She saw no traffic signals and only a few mud-spat-

91

tered cars. Even though it was only thirty miles from Juarez, the city where the church group was staying, the little village had none of the big city's civilized amenities. The people lived in stark poverty. Their homes were made of mud and tin and anything else they could find. There was no plumbing.

"Where do the people worship now?" she asked someone from her group.

"They meet here in the street," was the answer.

Pastor Burkhardt was right. The days were long and the work was hard. Each day for two weeks, they drove over terrible roads to the little village. Finally, a small, single room, concrete building sat at the end of the main street.

Working with the villagers had been an unexpected blessing for Sheila. Even though they spoke little English and she spoke no Spanish, she could see that they were kind and gracious people. More than once, one of the villagers had taken her

hand and quietly prayed for her as
she worked.

Even at that, Sheila's greatest blessing
was yet to come. On their last day in the
small town, a service was held in the new
church. A few chairs were distributed
about the room, but most sat on blankets
on the floor. The villagers sang with fervor
and spent much time in enthusiastic
prayer. Sheila sat quietly observing. The
church they seemed so grateful to have
was nothing like the beautiful, spacious

church she was used to at home, with its soft pews and carpeted floors.

"How can they be satisfied with so little?" she whispered to the Lord. Just then she looked up and could not believe what she was seeing. Two angels stood, with wings outspread in the front of the church just behind the altar. Two more stood in the back.

Sheila only saw the angels for a few moments, but she sensed their presence throughout the service. And she knew that God had given her the answer to her question. Who could ask for more than the privilege of worshipping God in the presence of his holy angels? It transformed even the crude building into the Sanctuary of God.[16]

*With Angels and Archangels, and with all the company of heaven, we laud and magnify thy glorious Name; evermore praising thee, and saying, Holy, holy, holy, Lord God of hosts, heaven and earth are full of thy glory: Glory be to thee, O Lord most High.*
THE BOOK OF COMMON PRAYER

# Angels Worship God

*Ye holy angels bright,*
*Who wait at God's right hand,*
*Or through the realms of light*
*Fly at your Lord's command,*
*Assist our song,*
*Or else the theme*
*Too high doth seem*
*For mortal tongue.*

JOHN HAMPDEN GURNEY

*All the angels were standing around the
throne and around the elders and the
four living creatures. They fell down
on their faces before the throne and
worshiped God, saying: "Amen! Praise and
glory and wisdom and thanks
and honor and power and strength be
to our God for ever and ever.
Amen!"*

REVELATION 7:11–12

# ANGELS CARRY OUT
*the Purposes of God*

In speaking of the angels, God says, "He
makes his angels winds, his servants
flames of fire."

HEBREWS 1:7

Angels take different forms at the bidding
of their master, God, and thus reveal
themselves to men and unveil the divine
mysteries to them.

SAINT JOHN OF DAMASCUS

# ANGELS PERFORM
# THEIR DUTIES

I [the Apostle John] saw four angels standing at the four corners of the earth, holding back the four winds so that no wind should blow on the earth or the sea or against any tree. And I saw another angel coming up from the east with the seal of the living God. He called out in a loud voice to the four angels to whom God had given the power to damage the earth and the sea. The angel said, "Do not harm the earth, the sea, or the trees, until we mark the servants of our God with a seal on their foreheads." And I was told that the number of those who were marked with God's seal on their foreheads was 144,000. They were from the twelve tribes of Israel, twelve thousand from each tribe: Judah, Reuben, Gad, Asher, Naphtali, Manasseh, Simeon, Levi, Issachar, Zebulun, Joseph, and Benjamin.

When the Lamb broke open the seventh seal, there was silence in heaven for about half an hour. Then I saw the seven angels who stand before God, and they were given seven trumpets.

Another angel, who had a gold incense container, came and stood at the altar. He was given a lot of incense to add to the prayers of all God's people and to offer it on the gold altar that stands before the throne. The smoke of the burning incense went up with the prayers of God's people from the hands of the angel standing before God. Then the angel took the incense container, filled it with fire from the altar, and threw it on the earth. There were rumblings and peals of thunder, flashes of lightning, and an earthquake.

Then the seven angels with the seven trumpets prepared to blow them.[17]

*There are two angels; that attend unseen*
*Each one of us, and in great books record*
*Our good and evil deeds. He who writes down*

The Gift of Angels

*The good ones, after every action closes*
*His volume, and ascends with it to God.*
*The other keeps his dreadful*
    *day-book open*
*Till sunset, that we may repent;*
    *which doing,*
*The record of the action fades away,*
*And leaves a line of white across the page.*

HENRY WADSWORTH LONGFELLOW

*Praise the LORD, all you heavenly powers,*
    *You servants of his, who do his will!*

PSALM 103:21 GNT

# THE HITCHHIKER

Reverend Dwyan Calvert felt exhilarated as he climbed into his blue Nova and started down the highway. Along with a number of other ministers from the area, he had spent the last twenty-seven hours in prayer.

Together the men had poured out their hearts, interceded for the people of the area in general and their own congregations in particular, and worshiped

God with great enthusiasm. Now it was 2:30 a.m., and Reverend Calvert was just now leaving Lubbock on his way back to Muleshoe, Texas. There were thirty-five miles of dark, moonless, west Texas highway between him and home. But Dwyan didn't care. He was happy to spend the time singing and praising God.

The first half of the ride to Muleshoe was uneventful, the highway deserted, the night still. Whether it was the darkness or his own reverie, Dwyan didn't notice the car pulled over on the shoulder until it was only a few yards ahead. He slowed down and saw that two men were working on the car's passenger side, perhaps changing a tire.

Dwyan thought about stopping, but quickly discarded the idea. After all, the men seemed to be working on the problem, and no one would argue that it could be dangerous to stop to help strangers on a deserted highway in the middle of the night.

On down the road, Dwyan tried to return to his happy disposition and songs of praise, but instead of jubilation, he was feeling a tug at his heart. *Wouldn't anyone be reluctant to stop at this hour?* He asked himself again. But the unsettling inner tug would not go away.

"Lord," he prayed, trying to find his way back to his exuberant former self, "you know that could have been a dangerous situation. Who knows what those people were up to? Besides, it's too late to turn back. I'm sure they will all be fine."

With that, Dwyan started singing his favorite worship song, but didn't feel any better. Finally, in desperation, he prayed, "Lord, I see now that I should have opened my heart to those people. They needed my help, and I drove right past. I give you my word that will not happen again. No matter how dark and how late, the next time I see someone who needs my help, I'll stop."

The words had barely passed his lips

when a man stepped from the darkness and waved. Dwyan saw no car on the shoulder, no house nearby. Nevertheless, he quickly stopped the car and backed to where the stranger was standing.

The man made his way quickly to the passenger door and hopped in without being formally asked.

"Hi, I'm Reverend Calvert," Dwyan said, offering his hand.

"Hello to you," the man responded. "I've been expecting you."

"Where are you headed?" Dwyan asked, puzzling over the man's strange reply.

"Just up here a ways," the man answered.

The two rode along quietly for a few miles before the man asked, "Where have you been tonight?"

"A prayer meeting," Dwyan responded.

The man nodded in a friendly manner, but said nothing.

When they reached the town of Sudan, Texas, the stranger told Dwyan that he could let him out near the square of the little town. When Dwyan dropped him off, the man shook his hand and thanked him for stopping.

Dwyan could see the man standing under the streetlight as he drove back onto the highway. He'd already gotten the point. God had sent an angel to remind him that serving him was more than high-minded words and spiritual activities. Serving God means reaching out beyond your fears, beyond your convenience, beyond your own personal agenda. It means actions as well as words. Reverend Calvert spent the rest of the trip worshipping God quietly and asking for a humble, tender heart toward the world around him.[18]

*Since we are surrounded by such a great cloud of witnesses, let us throw off everything that hinders and the sin that so easily entangles, and let us run with perseverance the race marked out for us.*

HEBREWS 12:1

# The Gift of Angels

*Make yourself familiar with the angels, and behold them frequently in spirit, for without being seen, they are present with you.*
SAINT FRANCIS DE SALES

*God will send his angels with a loud trumpet call, and they will gather his elect from the four winds, from one end of the heavens to the other.*
MATTHEW 24:31

*And yet, as angels in some brighter dreams*
*Call to the soul when man doth sleep,*
*So some strange thoughts transcend*
*Our wonted themes. And into glory peep.*

HENRY VAUGHN

# THE ANGEL OF
*the Lord*

*The angel of the LORD encamps around
those who fear him, and he delivers them.*

PSALM 34:7

*In Scripture we uniformly read that angels
are heavenly spirits, whose obedience and
ministry God employs to execute all the
purposes. which he has decreed, and hence
their name as being a kind of intermedi-
ate messenger to manifest his will to men.*

JOHN CALVIN

*Christians should never fail to sense the operation of an angelic glory. It forever eclipses the world of demonic powers, as the sun does a candle's light.*

BILLY GRAHAM

## THE ANGEL OF THE LORD WATCHES OVER ISAAC

When Abraham and Isaac reached the place God had told him about, Abraham built an altar there and arranged the wood on it. He bound his son Isaac and laid him on the altar, on top of the wood. Then he reached out his hand and took the knife to slay his son. But the angel of the LORD called out to him from heaven, "Abraham! Abraham!"

"Here I am," he replied.

"Do not lay a hand on the boy," he said. "Do not do anything to him. Now I know that you fear God, because you have not withheld from me your son, your only son."[19]

# THE ANGEL OF THE LORD ASCENDS IN A FLAME

Manoah said to the angel of the LORD, "We would like you to stay until we prepare a young goat for you."

The angel of the LORD replied, "Even though you detain me, I will not eat any of your food. But if you prepare a burnt offering, offer it to the LORD." (Manoah did not realize that it was the angel of the LORD.)

Then Manoah inquired of the angel
of the LORD, "What is your name, so
that we may honor you when your word
comes true?"

He replied, "Why do you ask my
name? It is beyond understanding." Then
Manoah took a young goat, together with
the grain offering, and sacrificed it on a
rock to the LORD. And the LORD did an
amazing thing while Manoah and his wife
watched: As the flame blazed up from the
altar toward heaven, the angel of the

LORD ascended in the flame. Seeing this, Manoah and his wife fell with their faces to the ground. When the angel of the LORD did not show himself again to Manoah and his wife, Manoah realized that it was the angel of the LORD.[20]

# ANGELS ARE THE CHOSEN AMBASSADORS OF GOD

*Announcing his coming*
*Just as the buglers go before*
*Announcing the arrival of the king.*

ANDREA GARNEY

*I, Jesus, have sent my angel to give you this testimony for the churches, I am the Root and the Offspring of David, and the bright Morning Star.*

REVELATION 22:16

*Angels can fly*
*because they take*
*themselves lightly.*

G. K. CHESTERTON

# ACKNOWLEDGMENTS

1 *Safe from the Hand of Herod*, Matthew 2:1–5, 7–15.

2 *Midnight Visitor,* interview and writing by Elece Hollis, Morris, Oklahoma.

3 *God's Angel in the Fiery Furnace,* Daniel 3:24-28.

4 *Caught on the Tracks,* Marie Asner, Overland Park, Kansas.

5 Poem by Betsy Williams, used by permission.

6 Poem by Ed Strauss, used by permission.

7 *The Angel Gabriel Delivers a Message to Mary*, Luke 1:26-38.

8 *An Angel Announces the Resurrection,*

Matthew 28:1–6.

9 *Angel in a Khaki Suit,* interview and writing by Elece Hollis, Morris, Oklahoma.

10 *An Angel Ministers to Jesus,* Luke 22:39–44.

11 *Mailbox Angel,* interview and writing by Elece Hollis, Morris, Oklahoma.

12 *An Angel Tells Paul What Will Happen,* Acts 27:21–25.

13 *Words of Reconciliation,* Michele Marr, Huntington Beach, California.

14 *The Angel of the Lord Foretells of Samson,* Judges 13:3–5.

15 *Angels Surround the Throne of God,*

Revelation 4:1–11 GNT.

16 *The Tabernacle of God,* interview and writing by Rebecca Currington, Tulsa, Oklahoma.

17 *Angels Perform Their Duties,* Revelation 7:1–8; 8:1–6 NTGNT.

18 *The Hitchhiker,* Reverend Dwyan Calvert, Lufkin, Texas.

19 *The Angel of the Lord Watches over Isaac,* Genesis 22:9–12.

20 *The Angel of the Lord Ascends in a Flame,* Judges 13:15–21.

This book has been bound using handcraft methods and Smyth-sewn to ensure durability.

The dust jacket and interior were designed by Eric Horner.

The text was edited by Janice Jacobson and compiled by Rebecca Currington in conjunction with Snapdragon Editorial Group, Inc.

The text was set in Minion, Felix Titling MT, and Sackers Italian Script.